Mary
Our Mother

Mary Our Mother

Written by Rosa Maria Ramalho, FSP

Illustrated by Ivan Coutinho

Pauline
BOOKS & MEDIA
Boston

ISBN 0-8198-4964-2

ISBN 978-0-8198-4964-9

Originally published in Portuguese as *Aprender com Maria: a Mãe de Jesus e nossa também*, Rosa Ramalho © 2016 by Pia Sociedade Filhas de São Paulo—Paulinas Editora, São Paulo (Brasil).

Copyright © 2017, English translation and adaptation by Daughters of St. Paul

Published by Pauline Books & Media, 50 Saint Pauls Avenue, Boston, MA 02130–3491

Printed in the U.S.A.

MOM VSAUSAPEOILL7-610091 4964-2

www.pauline.org

Pauline Books & Media is the publishing house of the Daughters of St. Paul, an international congregation of women religious serving the Church with the communications media.

1 2 3 4 5 6 7 8 9   21 20 19 18 17

For angels, big and small.

And for my personal angels,

Aline and José

Hello, my name is Gabriel. I want you to meet a very special person. Her name is Mary. She is the daughter of Joachim and Ann. They live in the city of Nazareth.

Activity

All families are special. They are a treasure
we receive from God. Draw a picture of your
family in the beautiful picture frame.

This is Joseph. Mary has promised to be his wife. Joseph is a good and just man. He is a carpenter in Nazareth.

Activity

All professions are important and necessary for society. Draw a line between each professional and the object they use.

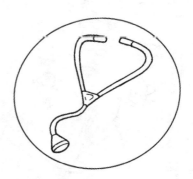

One day, God sent me to make a great announcement to Mary. I told her that God wanted her to be the Mother of Jesus, the Savior. Mary was not afraid to say "yes" to God's will.

Activity

Below is Mary's response. Color the letters.

"HERE AM I,
THE SERVANT
OF THE LORD;
LET IT BE WITH
ME ACCORDING TO
YOUR WORD."

LUKE 1:38

I told Mary that her elderly cousin Elizabeth was also expecting a baby. Mary left at once to go help her. Elizabeth was very happy. She told Mary that even the baby in her womb jumped for joy because Mary was carrying our Lord!

Activity

Mary's visit made Elizabeth and her baby very happy. Using good manners makes others happy too. Write the words we should use in the speech bubbles. Then color the pictures.

Thank you; I'm sorry; Excuse me

The emperor wanted all the people counted. To do this every person needed to return to the city their family came from. Since Joseph was from Bethlehem, Mary and Joseph traveled there.

BETHLEHEM

Activity

Find the road that will lead Joseph and Mary from Nazareth to Bethlehem.

So many people had traveled to Bethlehem that when Mary and Joseph arrived there was no place for them to stay. Mary told Joseph that the baby would be born soon. Finally, somebody let them stay in a stable where animals ate and were sheltered. That is where Jesus was born! Shepherds and some wise men from the East visited the Holy Family.

Activity

The wise men brought gold, frankincense, and myrrh as gifts for Jesus. What gift do you want to give Jesus? Draw or paste a picture of your gift in the space below.

When the wise men told King Herod that the King of the Jews had been born, Herod got jealous. He was afraid Jesus would be greater than him. King Herod wanted to prove he was the strongest king by hurting baby Jesus. God the Father sent an angel to Joseph in a dream to warn him of what the king wanted to do. So Joseph took Mary and Jesus to Egypt. After the king died, the Holy Family returned to Nazareth. There Jesus grew and learned many things from Mary and Joseph.

Activity

We can learn a lot from Jesus. In the word
search below look for some of Jesus' teachings.

FORGIVENESS   SERVICE

LOVE   COMPASSION

MERCY   SOLIDARITY

PRAYER   FAITH

P	R	S	K	Q	O	M	E	R	C	Y	K	C	S
Y	Z	B	E	I	I	R	W	P	G	I	L	O	O
P	Y	X	H	R	W	Q	M	G	N	S	D	M	L
Q	R	Y	H	I	V	A	V	W	T	U	N	P	I
O	W	A	X	G	L	I	S	V	C	G	N	A	D
J	O	K	Y	W	N	P	C	B	P	I	Y	S	A
O	V	I	L	E	N	T	R	E	H	E	W	S	R
L	O	V	E	F	R	D	J	K	U	Q	P	I	I
S	T	R	L	W	I	Y	F	A	I	T	H	O	T
V	F	O	R	G	I	V	E	N	E	S	S	N	Y

Jesus grew up and began his mission. He taught everyone how much God loves them and how to live as God wants. Jesus chose twelve men to follow him and learn from him. Mary was always close to her Son. She heard Jesus' words and put them into practice.

Activity

Do you know the names of Jesus' Apostles? Their names can be found in your Bible in Luke 6:12–16. Write them below.

_____   _____

_____   _____

_____   _____

_____   _____

_____   _____

Simon Peter, Andrew, James, John, Philip, Bartholomew, Matthew, Thomas, James son of Alphaeus, Simon the Zealot, Judas son of James, and Judas Iscariot

Sadly, not all the Apostles were faithful to Jesus. One of them betrayed Jesus and turned him over to those who wanted to kill Jesus because they did not believe in his teachings. Pontius Pilate condemned Jesus to crucifixion. This was Mary's greatest pain—a sword that pierced her chest.

On the Cross, Jesus turned to his mother and John, his disciple. Jesus said that from that day on Mary would be a mother to John and John would be a son to Mary.

Activity

This is a drawing of a famous sculpture called the *Pieta*. It shows the moment when Mary held her dead son in her arms after he was taken off the Cross. It was sculpted in 1489 by Michelangelo. Find out more about Michelangelo by searching the Internet.

On the third day, Jesus rose from the dead! Jesus lives—this is the reason for our great joy! Before Jesus ascended to Heaven he told his followers that God the Holy Spirit would soon come.

Activity

Fifty days after Jesus' resurrection, the Apostles and Mary were gathered in a room praying. The Holy Spirit came over them and filled them with God's love!

A dove is one symbol for the Holy Spirit. Follow the steps below to fold a sheet of paper and make an origami dove. Remember that the Holy Spirit helps us to love our neighbor and do good.

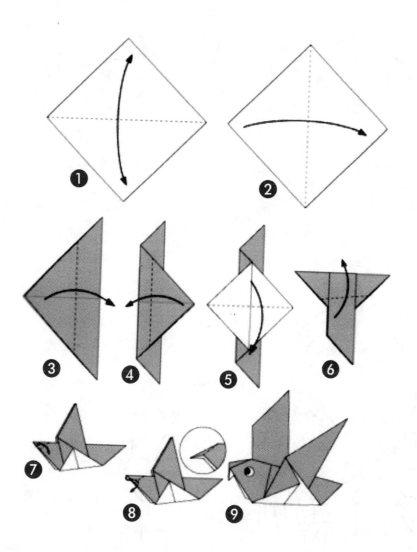

When Mary's time on earth was ending, she was taken up from the earth and assumed into heaven. She is Jesus' mother and our mother too! Mary is with God and from there she intercedes for us. This means that we can ask Mary to pray to God for us.

Apparitions of Our Lady

Since Jesus is Our Lord, we call Mary, Our Lady. Mary has appeared all over the world to help guide believers to follow her Son, Jesus.

Our Lady of Fatima
Portugal

Our Lady of Aparecida
Brazil

Our Lady of Guadalupe

Mexico

Our Lady of Lourdes
France

Our Lady of Mount Carmel

Holy Land

Praying with Mary

• • • • • • • • • • • • • • • • • •

Hail Mary

Hail Mary, full of grace, the Lord is with you. Blessed are you among women, and blessed is the fruit of your womb, Jesus. Holy Mary, Mother of God, pray for us sinners now and at the hour of our death. Amen.

Hail, Holy Queen

Hail, holy Queen, Mother of Mercy, our life, our sweetness, and our hope. To you we cry, poor banished children of Eve; to you we send up our sighs, mourning, and weeping in this valley of tears. Turn then, most gracious advocate, your eyes of mercy toward us, and after this our exile, show unto us the blessed fruit of your womb, Jesus. O clement, O loving, O sweet Virgin Mary. Pray for us, O holy Mother of God, that we may be made worthy of the promises of Christ. Amen.

Magnificat

(Mary's prayer in her cousin Elizabeth's house)

When the Virgin Mary visited her cousin Elizabeth, Mary responded to Elizabeth's greeting with this prayer of praise. The source of this prayer can be found in the Gospel of Luke 1:47–55.

36

My soul proclaims the greatness of the Lord,
my spirit rejoices in God, my Savior,
for you, Lord, have looked with favor on your lowly servant.
From this day all generations will call me blessed:
you, the Almighty, have done great things for me
and holy is your name.
You have mercy on those who fear you,
from generation to generation.
You have shown strength with your arm
and scattered the proud in their conceit,
casting down the mighty from their thrones,
and lifting up the lowly.
You have filled the hungry with good things
and sent the rich away empty.
You have come to the aid of your servant Israel,
to remember the promise of mercy,
the promise made to our forebears,
to Abraham and his children for ever.

Memorare

Remember, O most gracious Virgin Mary, that never was it known that anyone who fled to your protection, implored your help, or sought your intercession was left unaided. Inspired with this confidence, I fly to you, O Virgin of virgins, my Mother; to you do I come, before you I stand, sinful and sorrowful. O Mother of the Word Incarnate, despise not my petitions, but in your mercy hear and answer me. Amen.

Prayer to Mary, Mother of Jesus

Dear Mother of Jesus and my Mother too, I want to learn to love Jesus and do everything he taught. Take care of me, Mary, so that I never stop being a good person. Also take care of my family, my friends, and all people who suffer, especially children. I want to always follow your example and to always be on your lap and under your protection. Amen.

Pauline
BOOKS & MEDIA

The Daughters of St. Paul operate book and media centers at the following addresses. Visit, call, or write the one nearest you today, or find us at www.paulinestore.org.

CALIFORNIA
3908 Sepulveda Blvd, Culver City, CA 90230   310-397-8676
3250 Middlefield Road, Menlo Park, CA 94025   650-369-4230

FLORIDA
145 SW 107th Avenue, Miami, FL 33174   305-559-6715

HAWAII
1143 Bishop Street, Honolulu, HI 96813   808-521-2731

ILLINOIS
172 North Michigan Avenue, Chicago, IL 60601   312-346-4228

LOUISIANA
4403 Veterans Memorial Blvd, Metairie, LA 70006   504-887-7631

MASSACHUSETTS
885 Providence Hwy, Dedham, MA 02026   781-326-5385

MISSOURI
9804 Watson Road, St. Louis, MO 63126   314-965-3512

NEW YORK
115 E. 29th St., New Your City, NY 10016   212-754-1110

SOUTH CAROLINA
243 King Street, Charleston, SC 29401   843-577-0175

TEXAS
No book center; for parish exhibits or outreach evangelization, contact: 210-569-0500 or SanAntonio@paulinemedia.com or P.O. Box 761416, San Antonio, TX 78245

VIRGINIA
1025 King Street, Alexandria, VA 22314   703-549-3806

CANADA
3022 Dufferin Street, Toronto, ON M6B 3T5   416-781-9131

SMILE God loves you!